ABOUT KUMON

What is Kumon?

Kumon is the world's largest supplemental education provider and a leader in producing outstanding results. After-school programs in math and reading at Kumon Centers around the globe have been helping children succeed for 50 years.

Kumon Workbooks represent just a fraction of our complete curriculum of preschool-to-college-level material assigned at Kumon Centers under the supervision of trained Kumon Instructors.

The Kumon Method enables each child to progress successfully by practicing material until concepts are mastered and advancing in small, manageable increments. Instructors carefully assign materials and pace advancement according to the strengths and needs of each individual student.

Students usually attend a Kumon Center twice a week and practice at home the other five days. Assignments take about twenty minutes.

Kumon helps students of all ages and abilities master the basics, improve concentration and study habits, and build confidence.

How did Kumon begin?

IT ALL BEGAN IN JAPAN 50 YEARS AGO when a parent and teacher named Toru Kumon found a way to help his son Takeshi do better in school. At the prompting of his wife, he created a series of short assignments that his son could complete successfully in less than 20 minutes a day and that would ultimately make high school math easy. Because each was just a bit more challenging than the last, Takeshi was able to master the skills and gain the confidence to keep advancing.

This unique self-learning method was so successful that Toru's son was able to do calculus by the time he was in the sixth grade. Understanding the value of good reading comprehension, Mr. Kumon then developed a reading program employing the same method. His programs are the basis and inspiration of those offered at Kumon Centers today under the expert guidance of professional Kumon Instructors.

Mr. Toru Kumon
Founder of Kumon

What can Kumon do for my child?

Kumon is geared to children of all ages and skill levels. Whether you want to give your child a leg up in his or her schooling, build a strong foundation for future studies or address a possible learning problem, Kumon provides an effective program for developing key learning skills given the strengths and needs of each individual child.

What makes Kumon so different?

Kumon uses neither a classroom model nor a tutoring approach. It's designed to facilitate self-acquisition of the skills and study habits needed to improve academic performance. This empowers children to succeed on their own, giving them a sense of accomplishment that fosters further achievement. Whether for remedial work or enrichment, a child advances according to individual ability and initiative to reach his or her full potential. Kumon is not only effective, but also surprisingly affordable.

What is the role of the Kumon Instructor?

Kumon Instructors regard themselves more as mentors or coaches than teachers in the traditional sense. Their principal role is to provide the direction, support and encouragement that will guide the student to performing at 100% of his or her potential. Along with their rigorous training in the Kumon Method, all Kumon Instructors share a passion for education and an earnest desire to help children succeed.

KUMON FOSTERS:
- A mastery of the basics of reading and math
- Improved concentration and study habits
- Increased self-discipline and self-confidence
- A proficiency in material at every level
- Performance to each student's full potential
- A sense of accomplishment

▶▶ **GETTING STARTED IS EASY.** Just call us at 877.586.6671 or visit kumon.com to request our free brochure and find a Kumon Center near you. We'll direct you to an Instructor who will be happy to speak with you about how Kumon can address your child's particular needs and arrange a free placement test. There are more than 1,700 Kumon Centers in the U.S. and Canada, and students may enroll at any time throughout the year, even summer. Contact us today.

FIND OUT MORE ABOUT KUMON MATH & READING CENTERS.
Receive a free copy of our parent guide, *Every Child an Achiever*, by visiting kumon.com/go.survey or calling 877.586.6671

1 Out of the Deep

Name
Date

To parents Encourage your child to trace the path of the crab. It is okay if your child draws outside the designated area. The important thing is that your child draws slowly and carefully.

■ Draw a line from one crab ( ) to the other crab ().

■ Draw a line from one picture to the matching picture.

2 Slimy Trail

Name

Date

To parents This exercise teaches your child to draw curved lines. Encourage your child to move the pencil slowly along the curved path. Praise your child when he or she has completed the activity.

■ Draw a line from one slug ( ) to the other slug ( ).

3

■ Draw a line from one picture to the matching picture.

3 Spring in Your Step

Name

Date

To parents This exercise teaches your child to draw zigzag lines. This is often difficult for children. If drawing the whole line in one stroke is too difficult, your child may pause in the middle.

■ Draw a line from one grasshopper ( ) to the other grasshopper ( ).

■ Draw a line from one picture to the matching picture.

4 Soaring in the Sky

Name

Date

To parents It is okay if your child draws outside the designated area. Encourage your child to trace slowly and carefully.

■ Draw a line from one skydiver ( 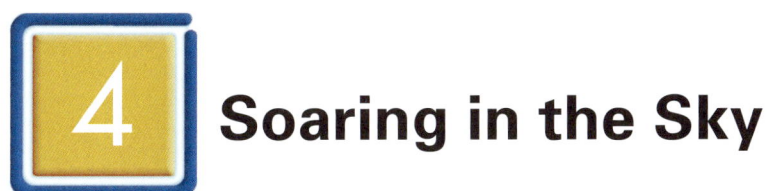) to the other skydiver ( ).

7

■ Draw a line from one picture to the matching picture.

5 Mowing the Lawn

Name

Date

To parents Encourage your child to draw steadily. When your child has finished, offer praise, such as "Great job!"

■ Draw a line from one lawn mower (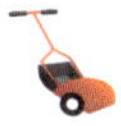) to the other lawn mower (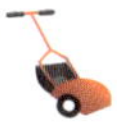).

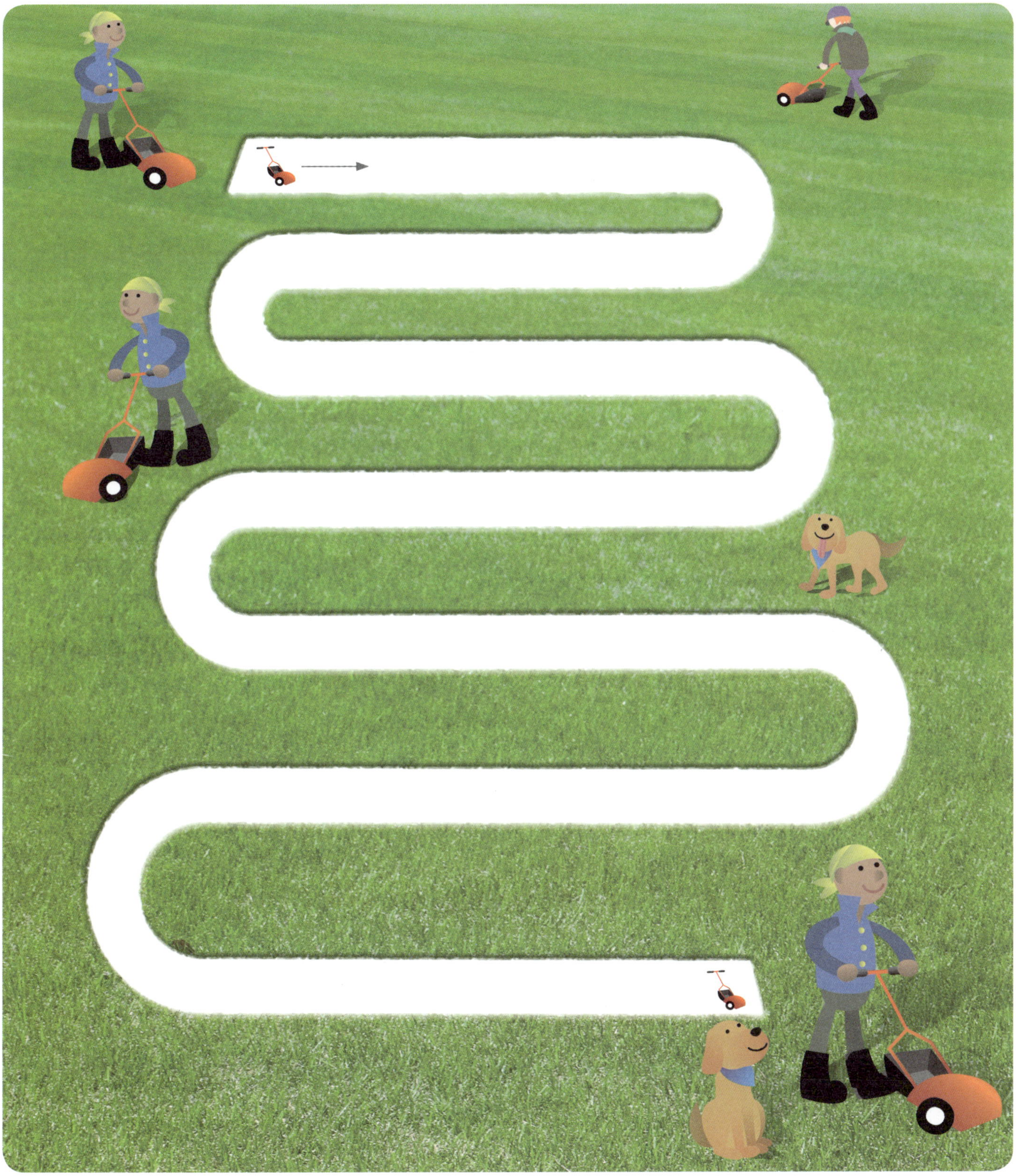

■ Draw a line from one picture to the matching picture.

6 Butterfly in the Sky

Name

Date

To parents Encourage your child to draw the path of the butterfly. Make sure your child follows the arrows at the crossing point so that he or she draws in the correct direction.

■ Draw a line from one butterfly ( ) to the other butterfly ().

■ Draw a line from one picture to the matching picture.

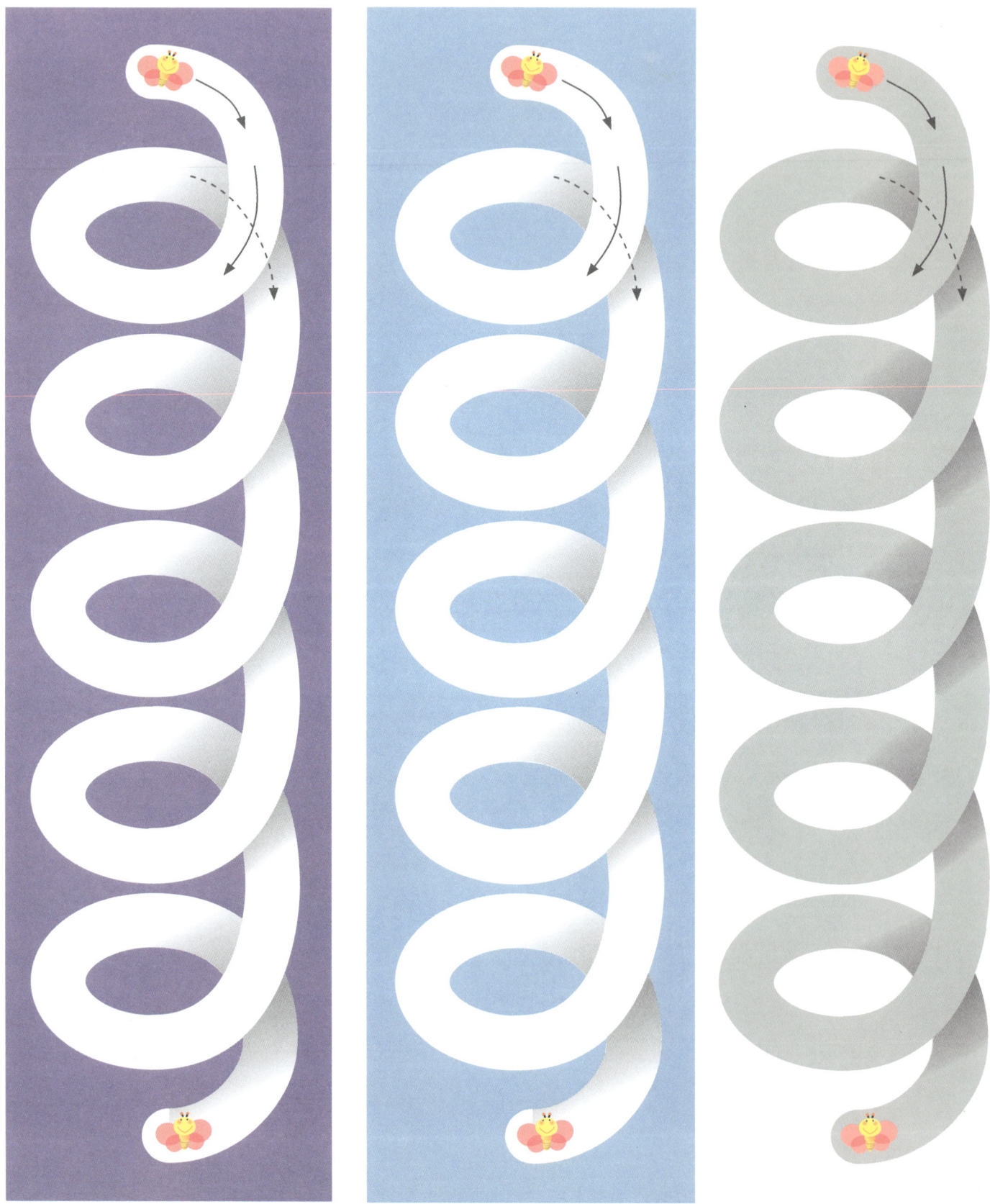

7 Garden Tunnel

■ Draw a line from one mole ( ) to the other mole ().

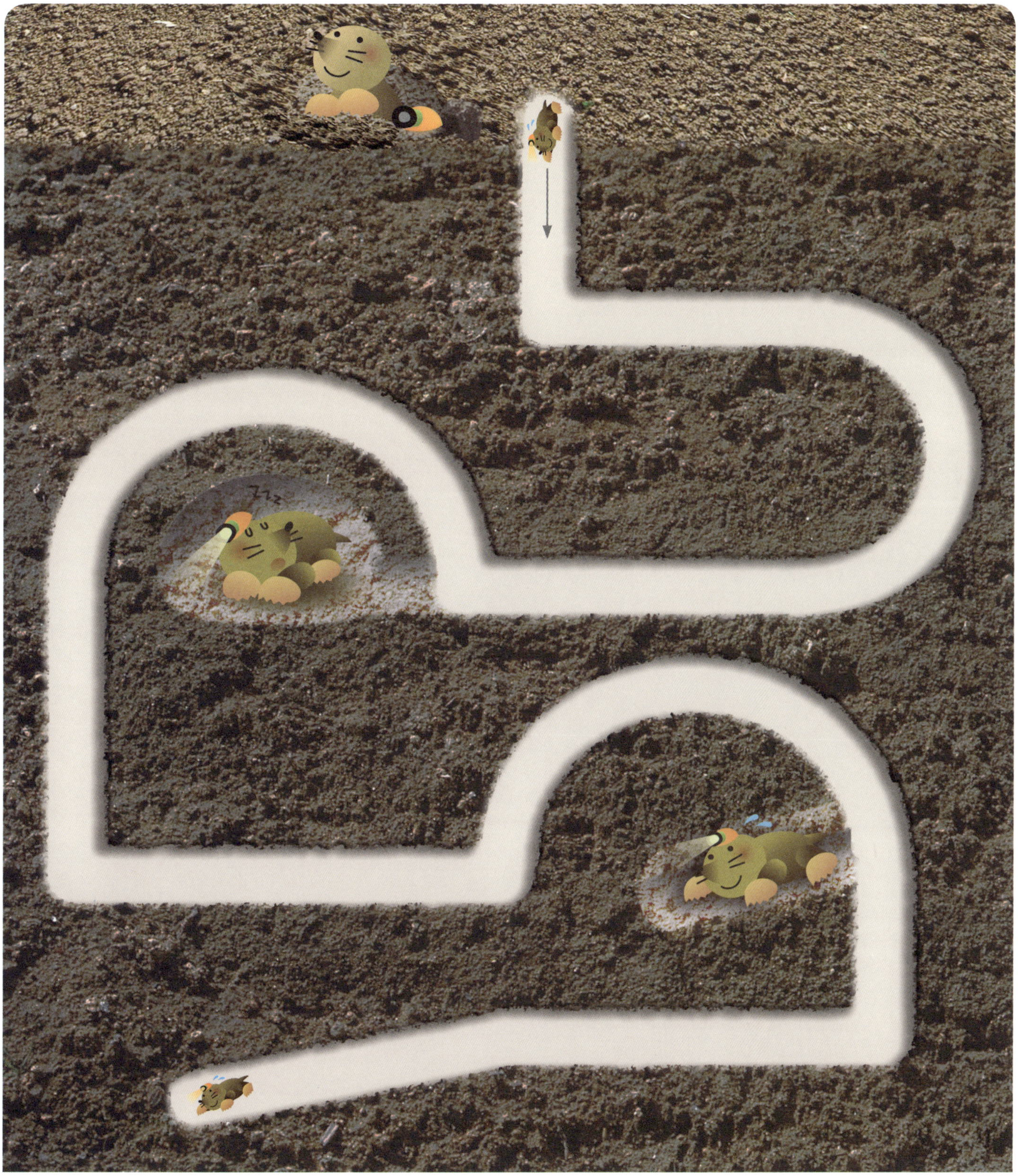

■ Draw a line from the dot (●) to the star (★).

Elephant

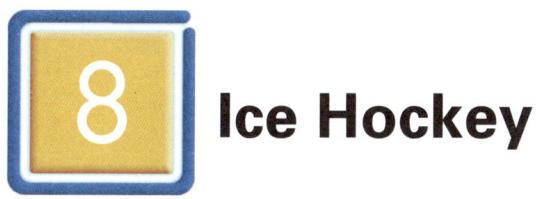

8 Ice Hockey

Name

Date

To parents From this page on, the starting point will be at different locations on the page. Please encourage your child to look carefully for the starting point before beginning to trace.

■ Draw a line from one puck (●) to the other puck (●).

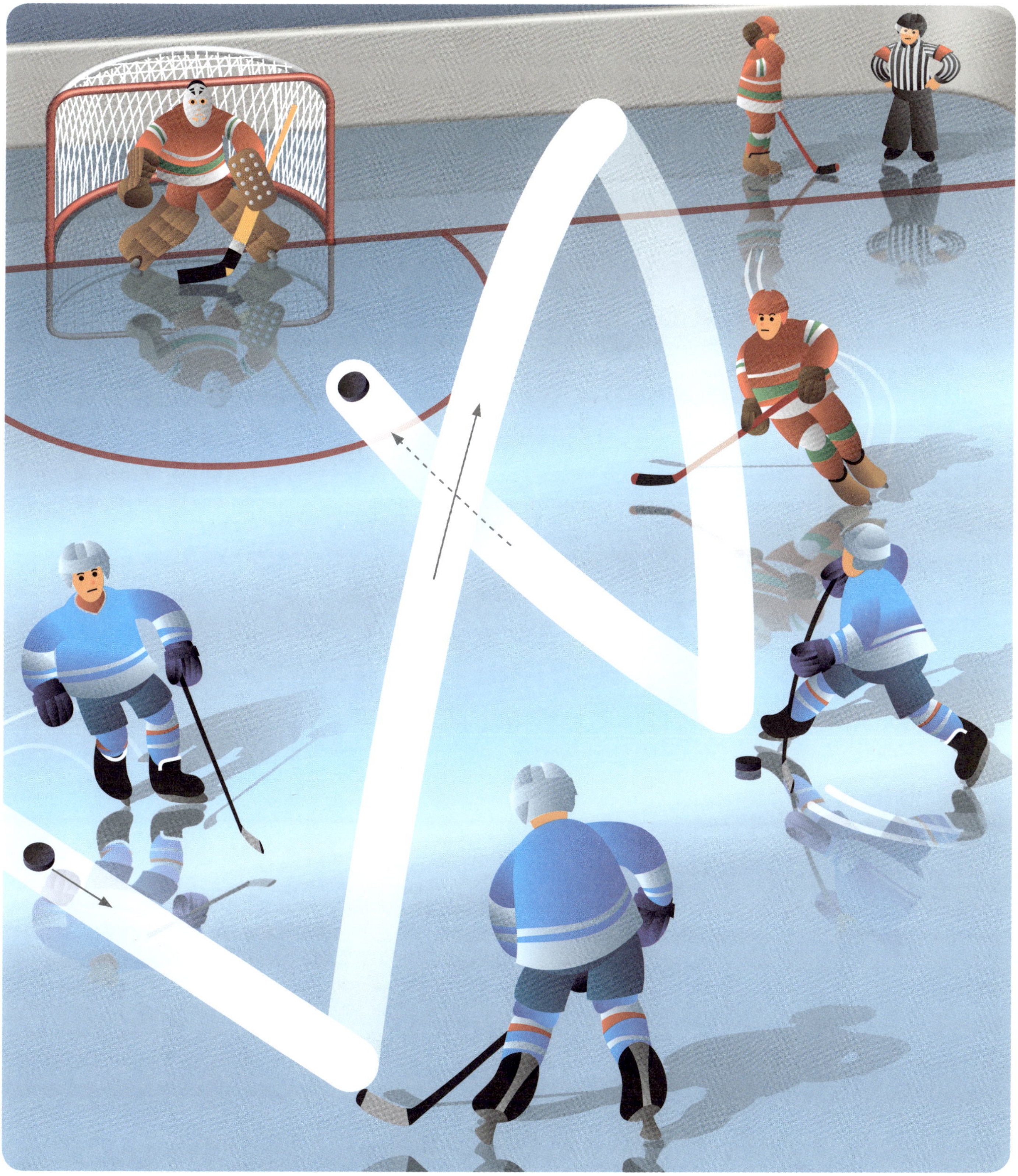

■ Draw a line from the dot (●) to the star (★).

Penguin

9 Men at Work

Name

Date

■ Draw a line from one cone (🚧) to the other cone (🚧).

17

■ Draw a line from the dot (●) to the star (★).

Orangutan

10 Underwater

Name
Date

■ Draw a line from one ray () to the other ray ( ).

■ Draw a line from the dot (●) to the star (★).

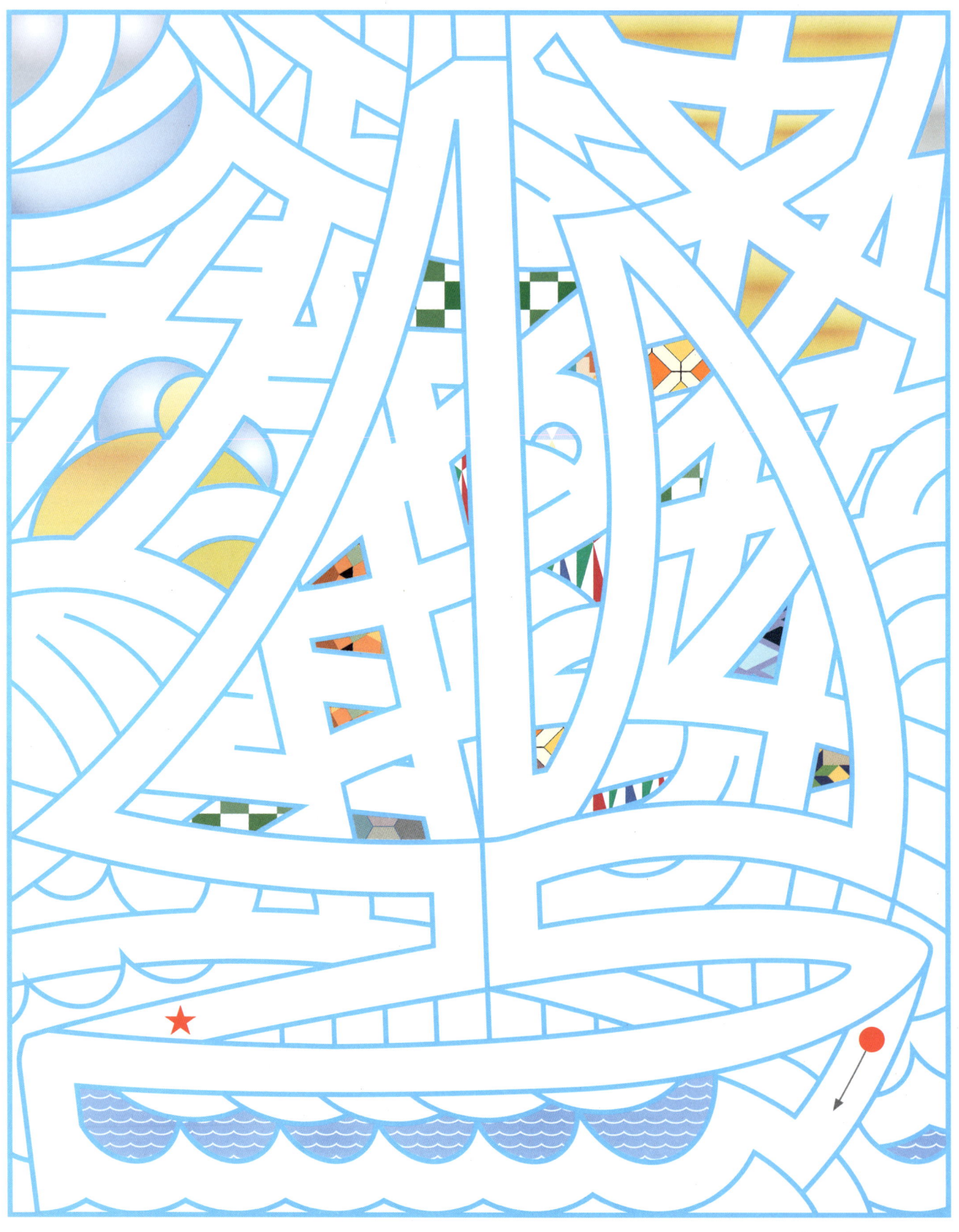

Sailboat

11 Hopping Home

■ Draw a line from one rabbit () to the other rabbit ( ).

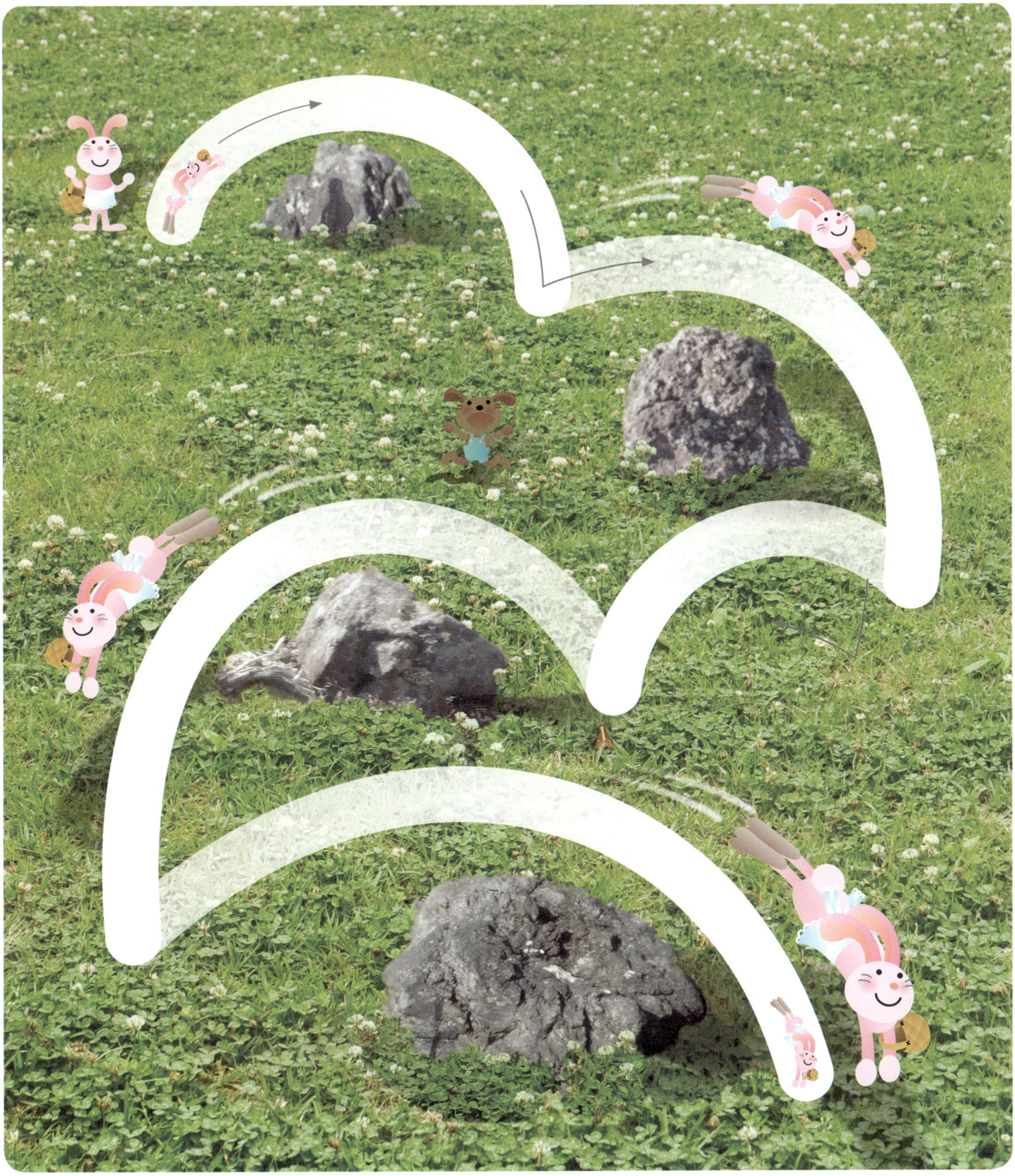

■ Draw a line from the dot (●) to the star (★).

Birthday Cake

12 Leap Frogs

■ Draw a line from one frog () to the other frog ( ).

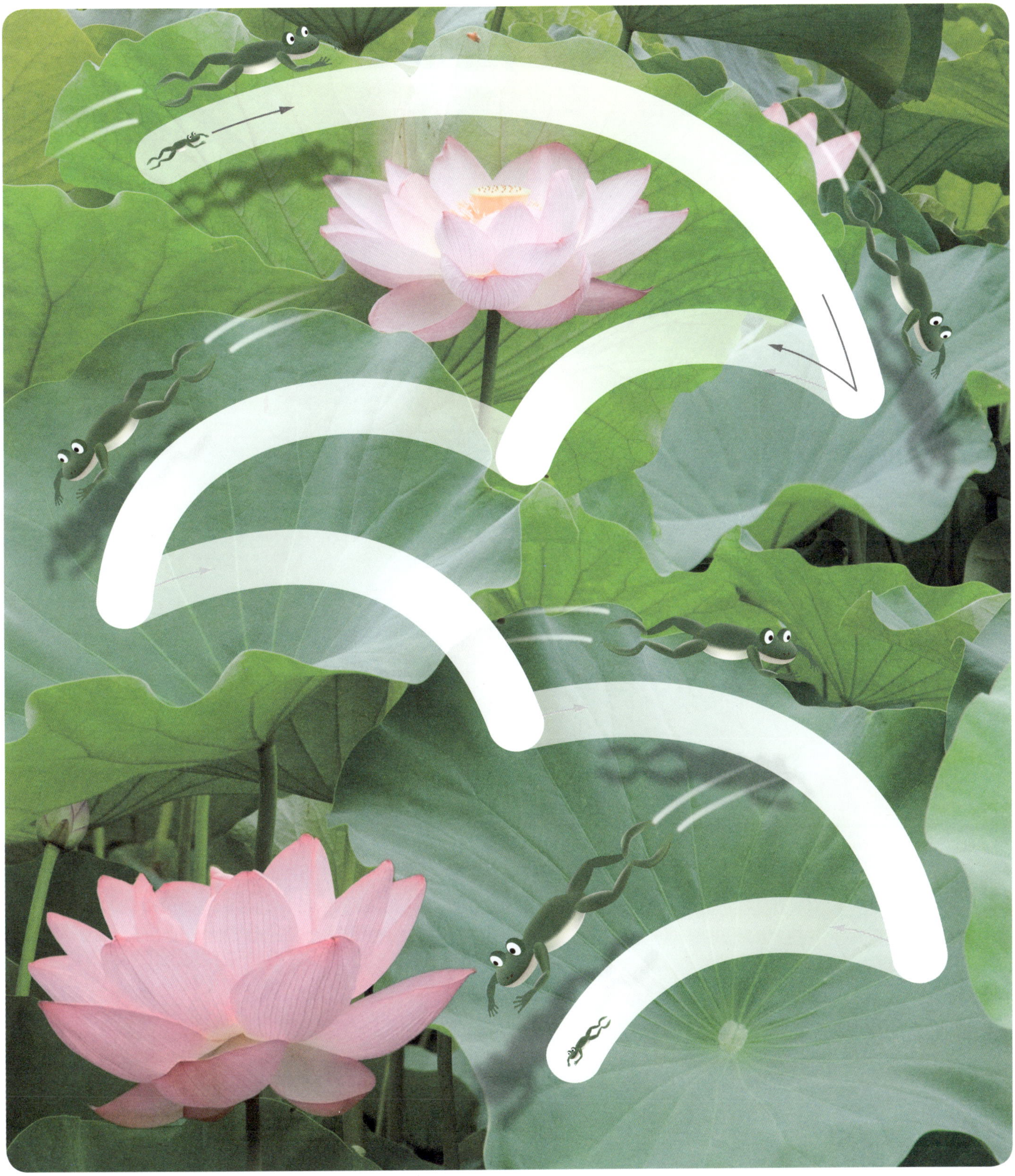

23

■ Draw a line from the dot (●) to the star (★).

Teapot

13 Clean the Chalkboard

Name

Date

To parents If drawing the whole line in one stroke is too difficult, your child may pause in the middle. When your child has completed the exercise, offer lots of praise.

■ Draw a line from one eraser ( ) to the other eraser ( ).

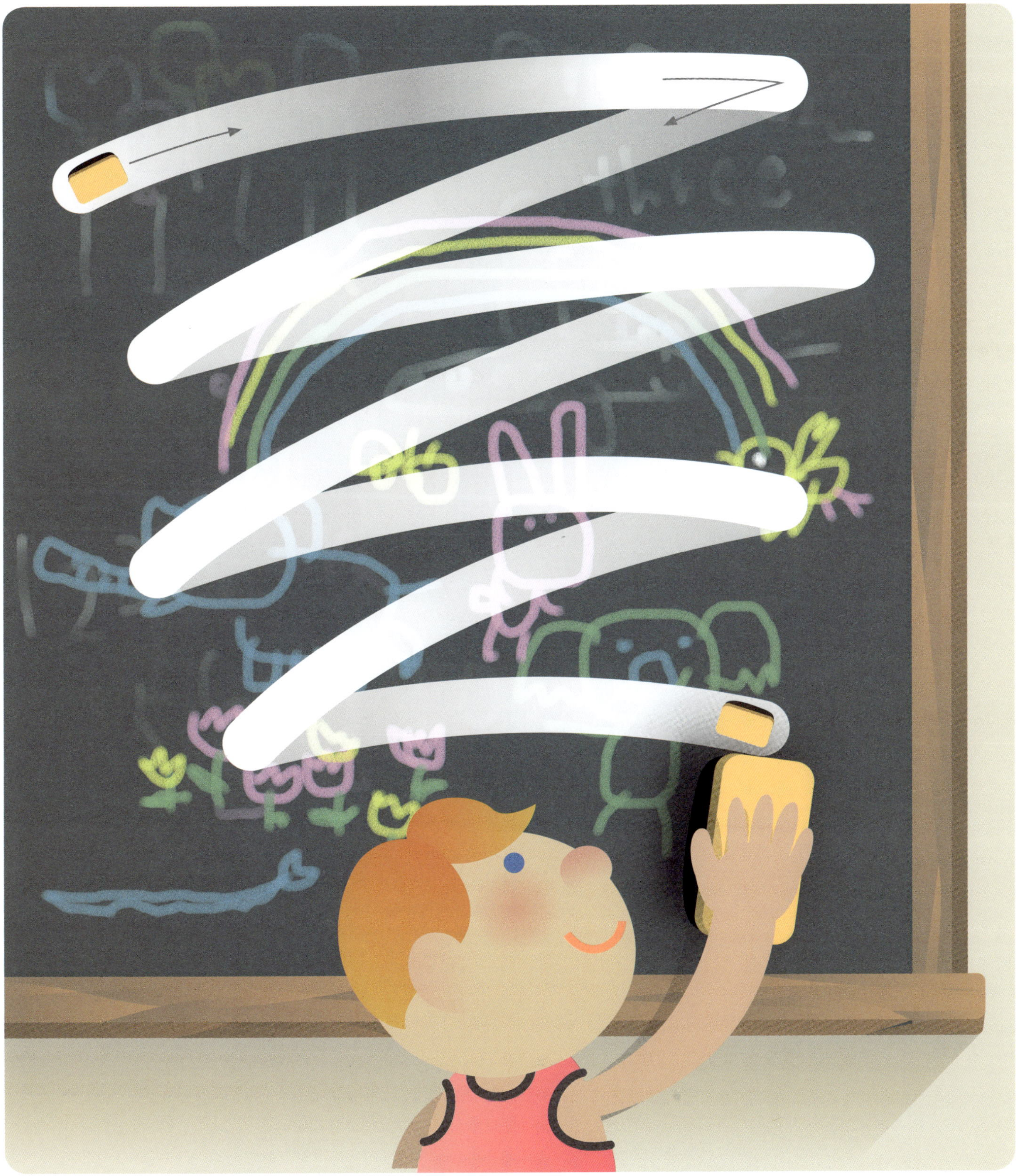

■ Draw a line from the dot (●) to the star (★).

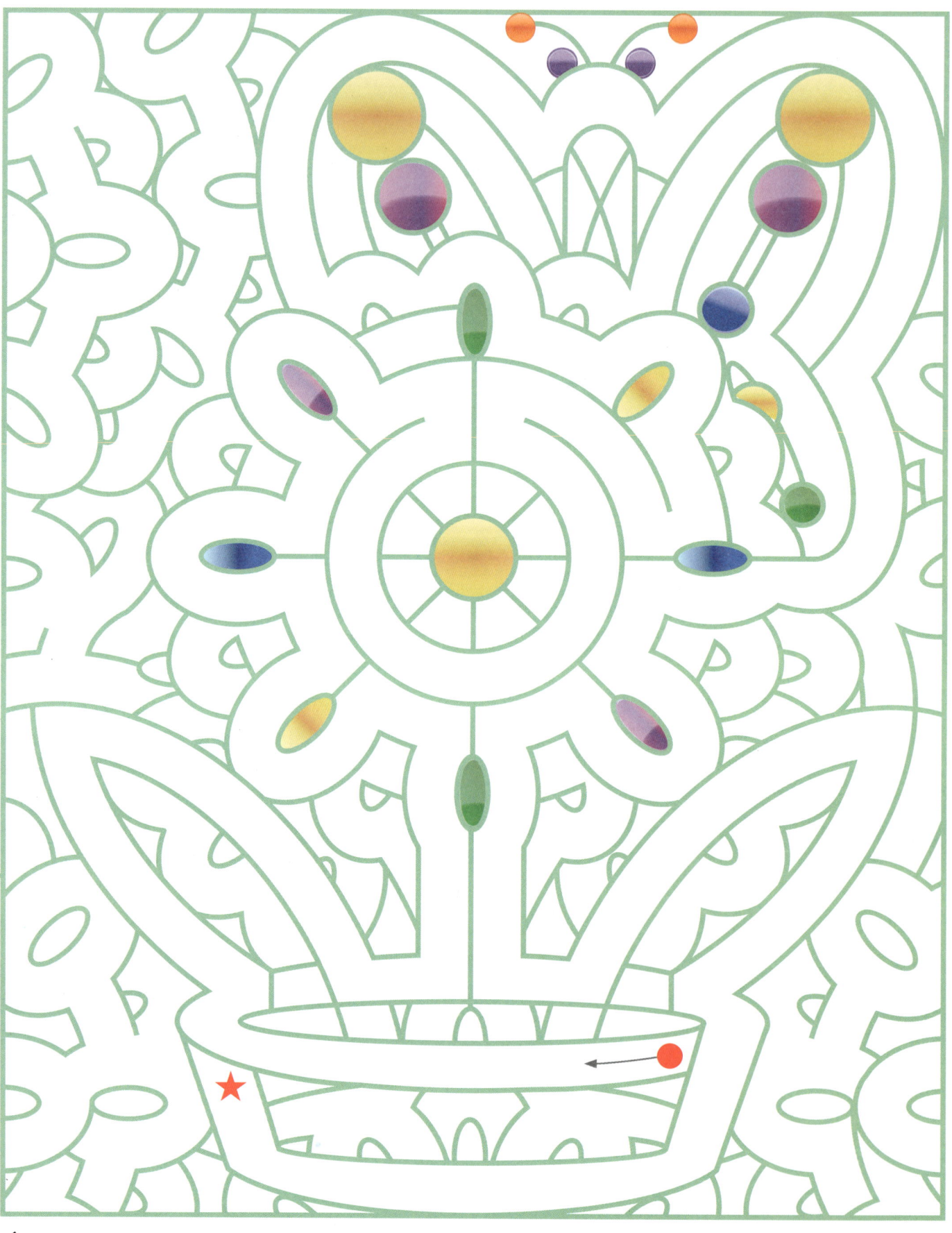

26 Butterfly and Flower

14 Tropical Trip

Name

Date

To parents From this page on, the paths are narrower. It is more important that your child draw slowly and carefully, rather than draw in one stroke.

■ Draw a line from one tortoise () to the other tortoise ().

27

■ Draw a line along the red path (❶) and then the blue path (❷).

15 Night Lights

Name

Date

To parents Encourage your child to draw the path of the firefly. Make sure your child follows the arrows at the crossing point so that he or she draws in the correct direction.

■ Draw a line from one firefly ( ) to the other firefly ( ).

29

■ Draw a line along the red path (❶) and then the blue path (❷).

16 Space Walk

Name

Date

- Draw a line from one astronaut (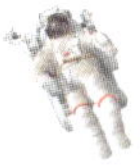) to the other astronaut (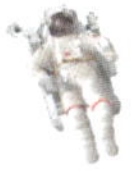).

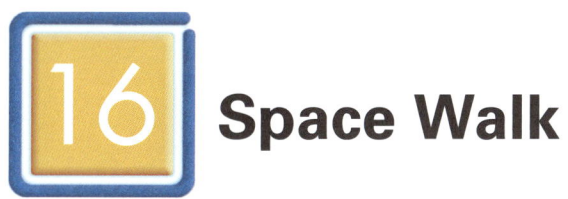

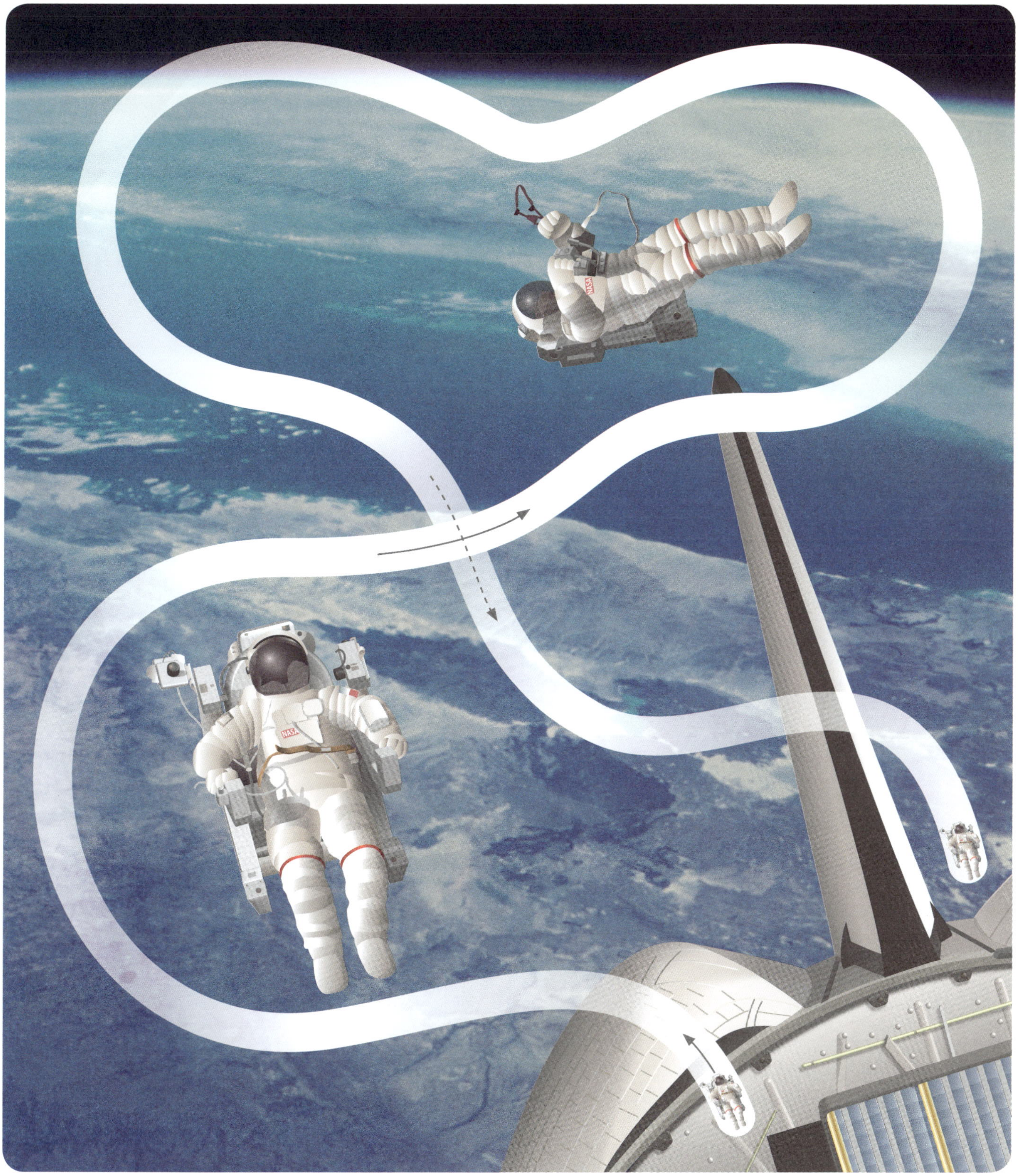

To parents Encourage your child to draw the lines in numerical order. These exercises will help his or her pencil-stroke skills for writing letters.

■ Draw a line along the red path (❶) and then the blue path (❷).

17 Teamwork

Name

Date

To parents
Encourage your child to draw slowly and carefully.

■ Draw a line from one ball () to the other ball ( ).

33

- Draw a line along the red path (❶), then the blue path (❷), and then the orange path (❸).

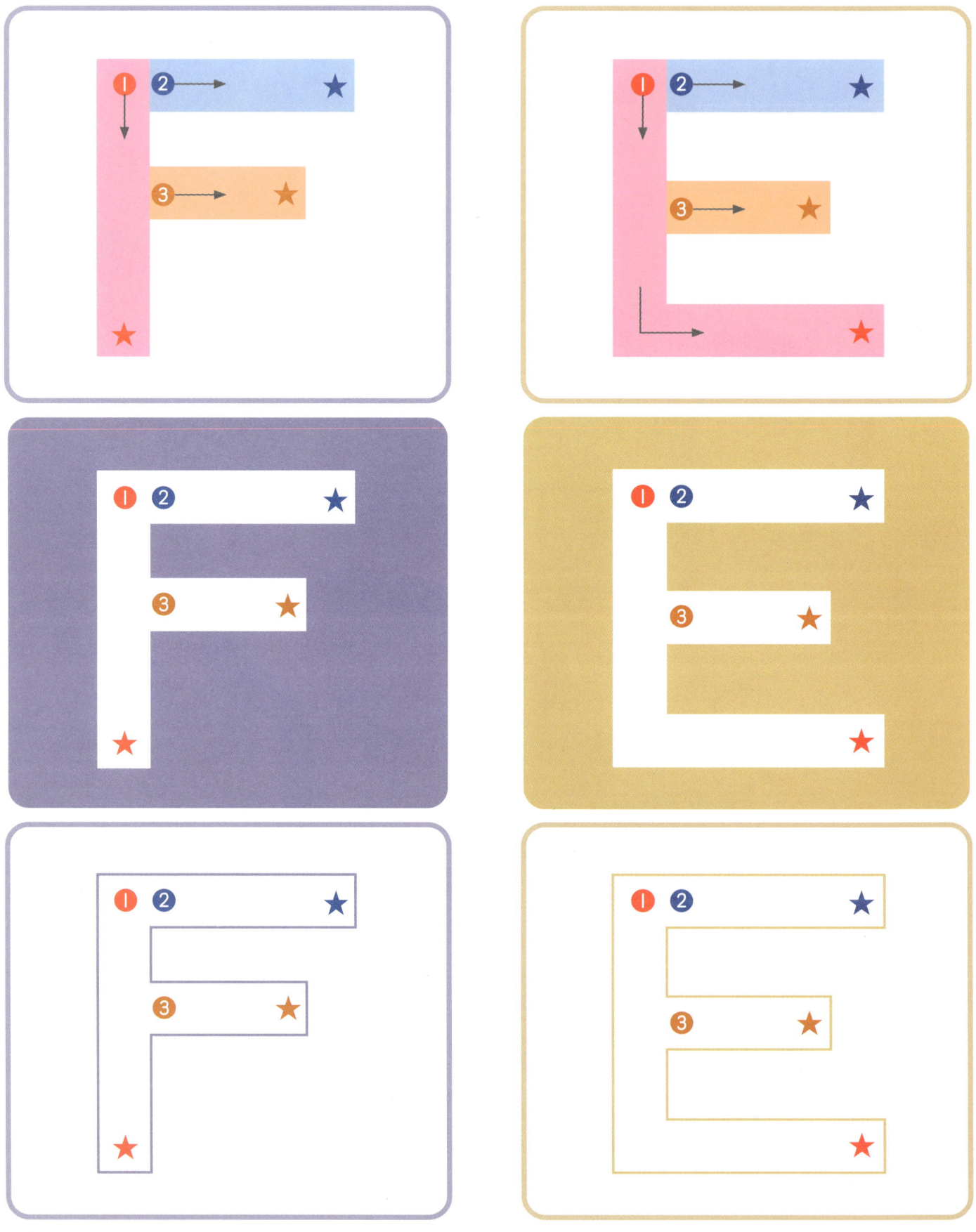

18 Table Hockey

Name
Date

To parents Encourage your child to draw the path of the puck. If your child is unsure of the path, please ask him or her to trace the line with his or her finger first.

■ Draw a line from one puck () to the other puck ( ).

35

■ Draw a line along the red path (❶), then the blue path (❷), and then the orange path (❸).

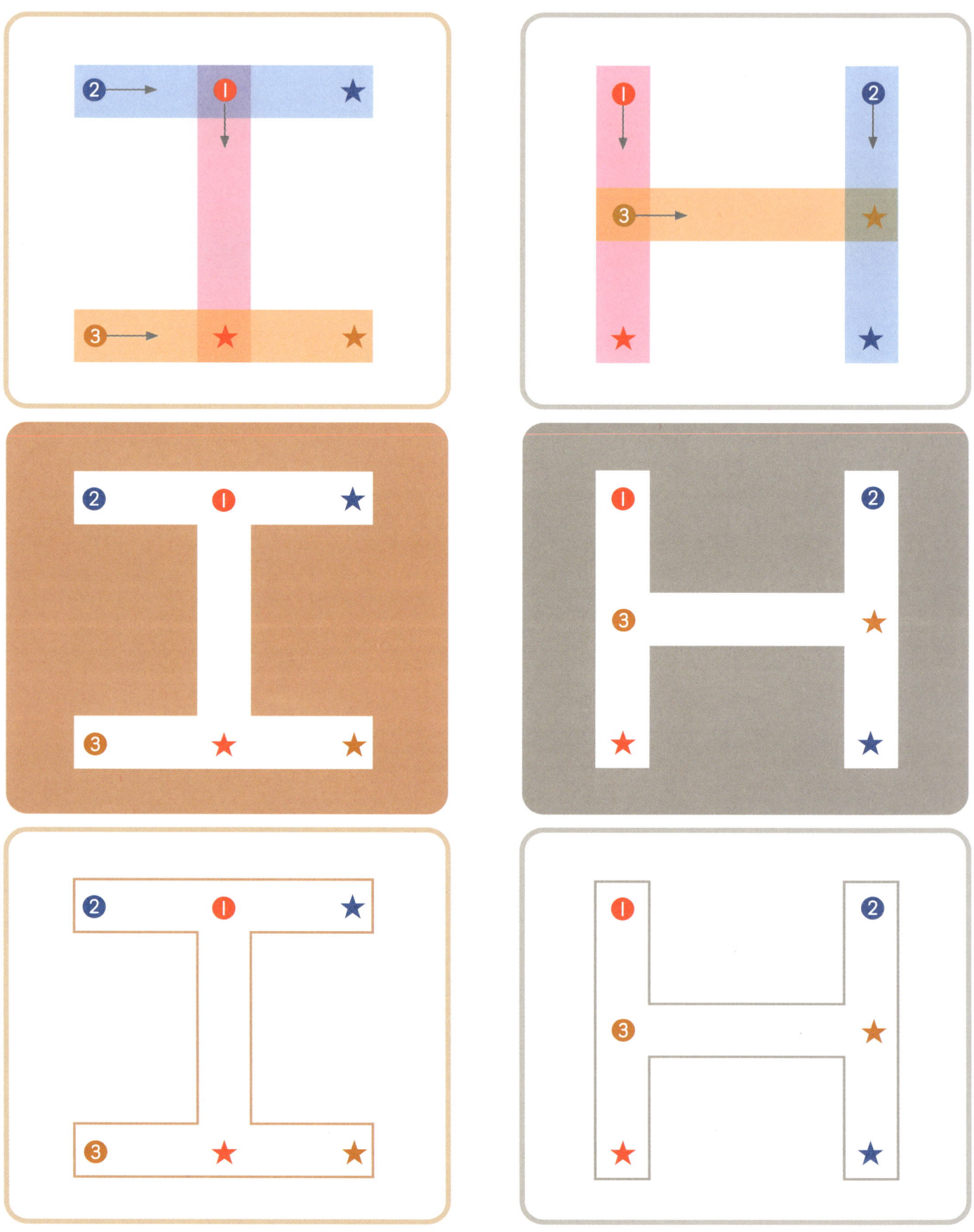

19 Pond Path

Name

Date

■ Draw a line from one water skimmer (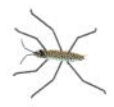) to the other water skimmer (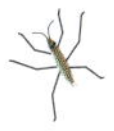).

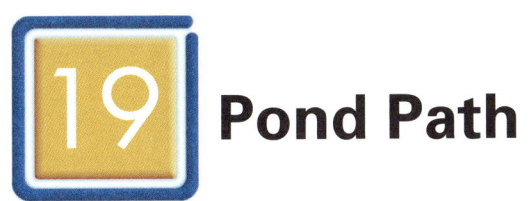

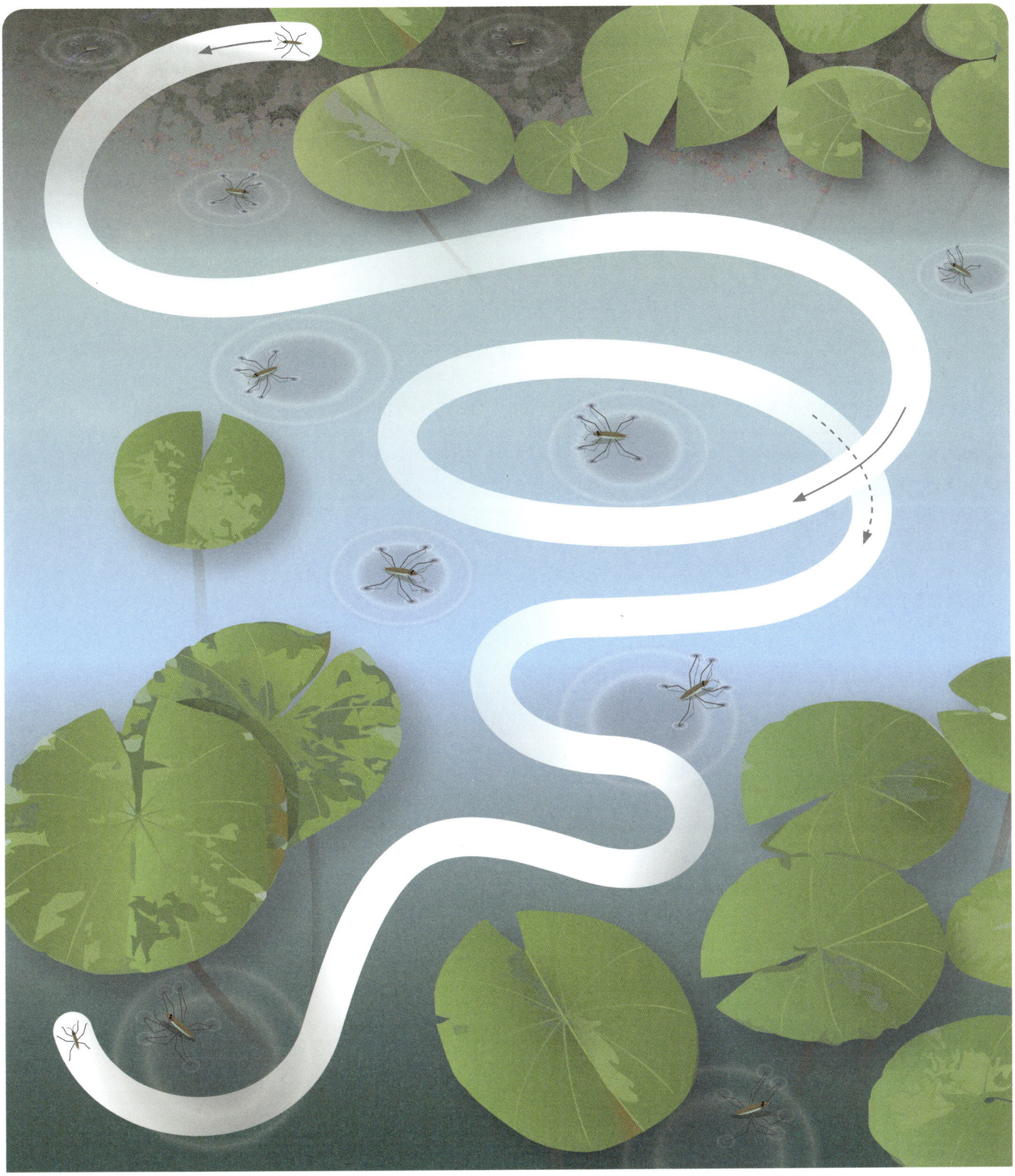

■ Draw a line from the dot (●) to the star (★).

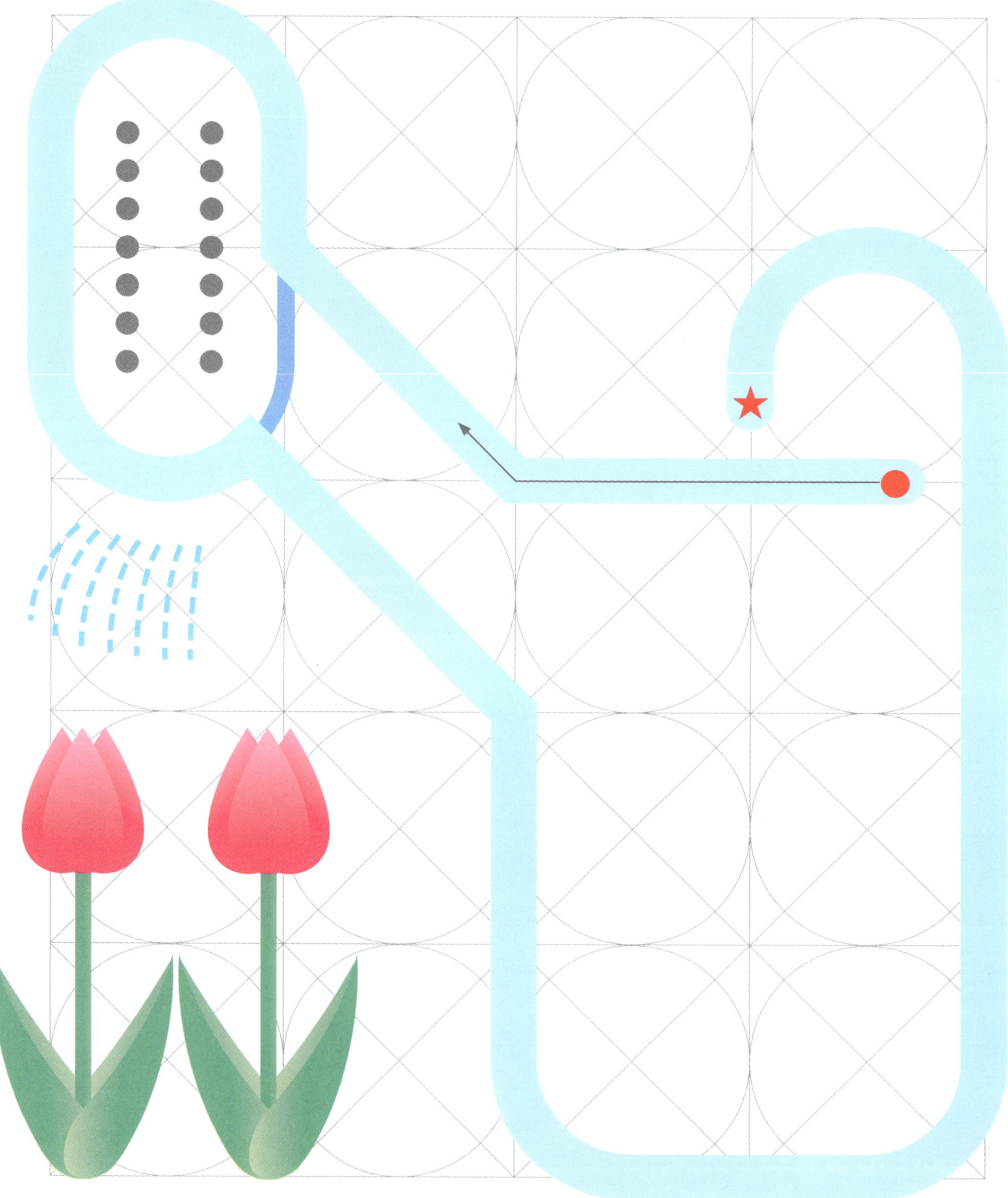

Watering Can

20 Fall Leaves

Name

Date

To parents When your child has finished, offer him or her praise and talk about his or her favorite season.

■ Draw a line from one leaf (🍂) to the other leaf (🍂).

■ Draw a line from the dot (●) to the star (★).

40

Camel

21 Tree Trunk Track

Name
Date

To parents Encourage your child to draw the path of the bug. If your child is unsure of the path, please ask him or her to trace the line with his or her finger first.

■ Draw a line from one bug ( ) to the other bug ( ).

41

■ Draw a line from the dot (●) to the star (★).

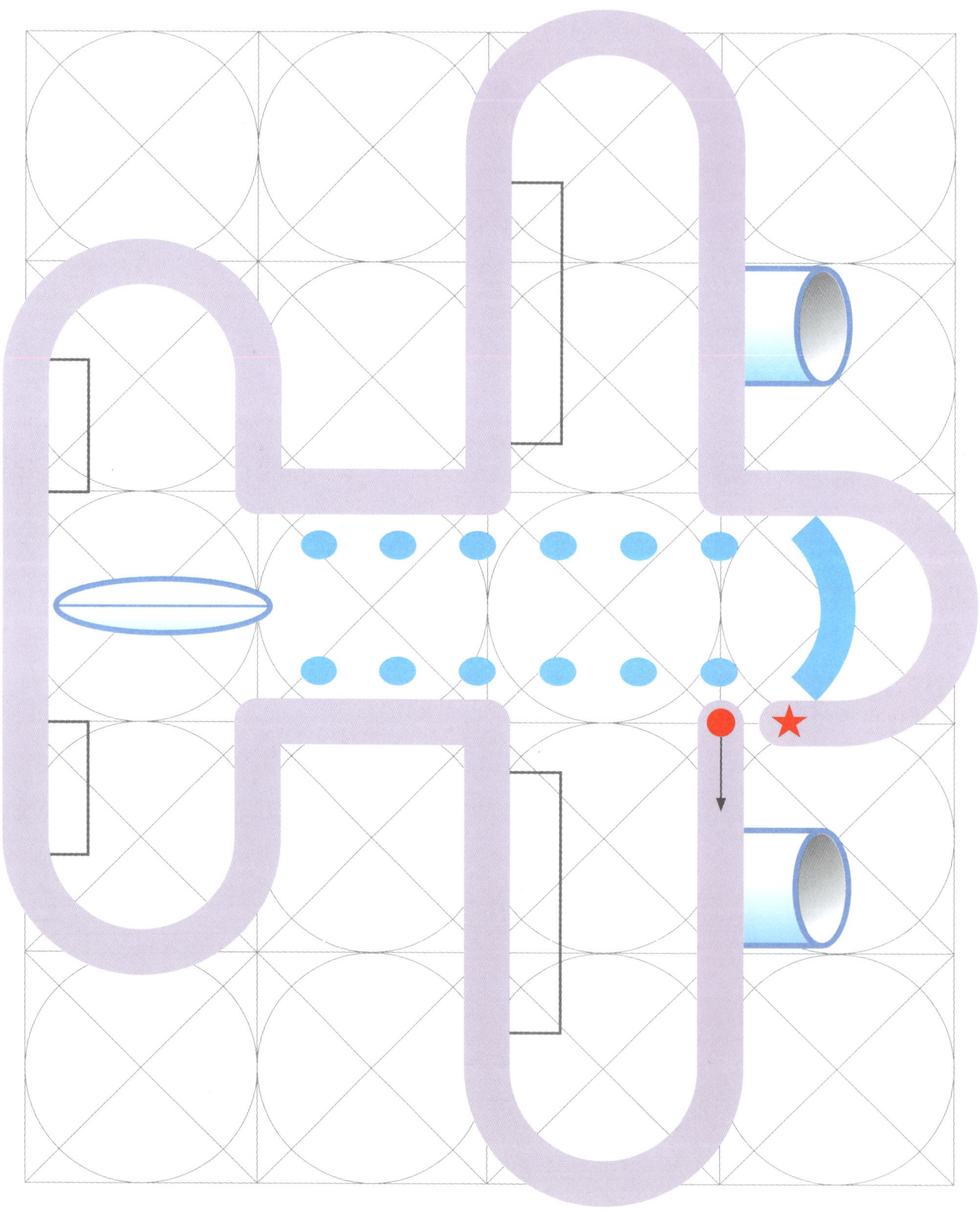

Airplane

22 Worming Around

Name

Date

■ Draw a line from one worm (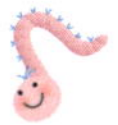) to the other worm (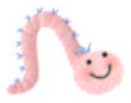).

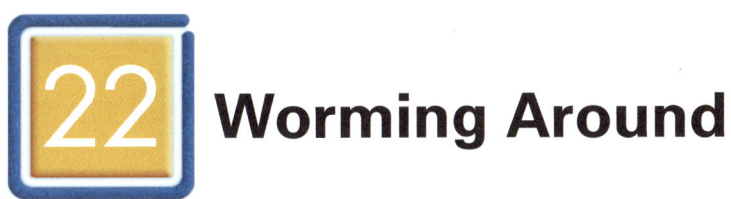

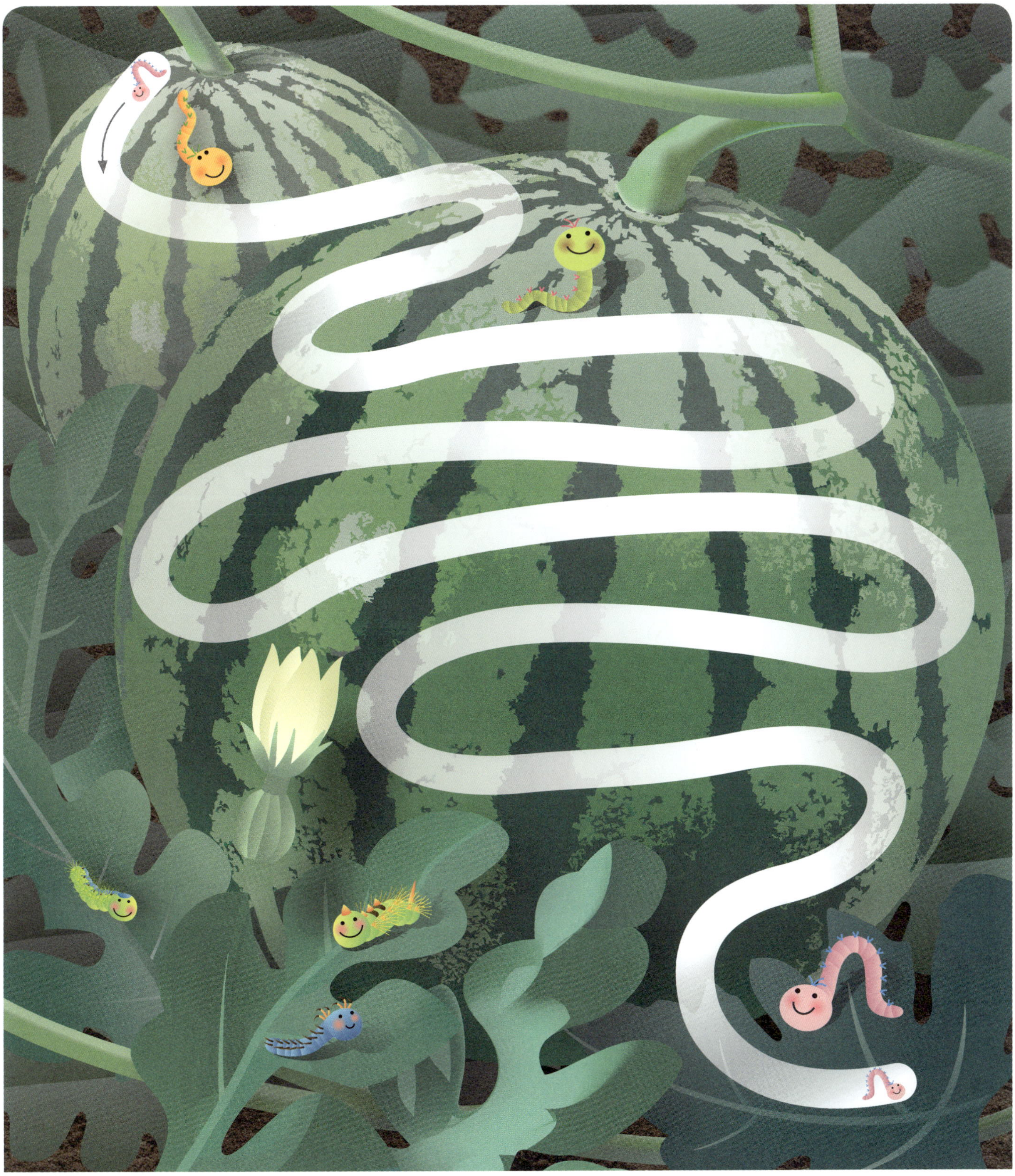

■ Draw a line from the dot (●) to the star (★).

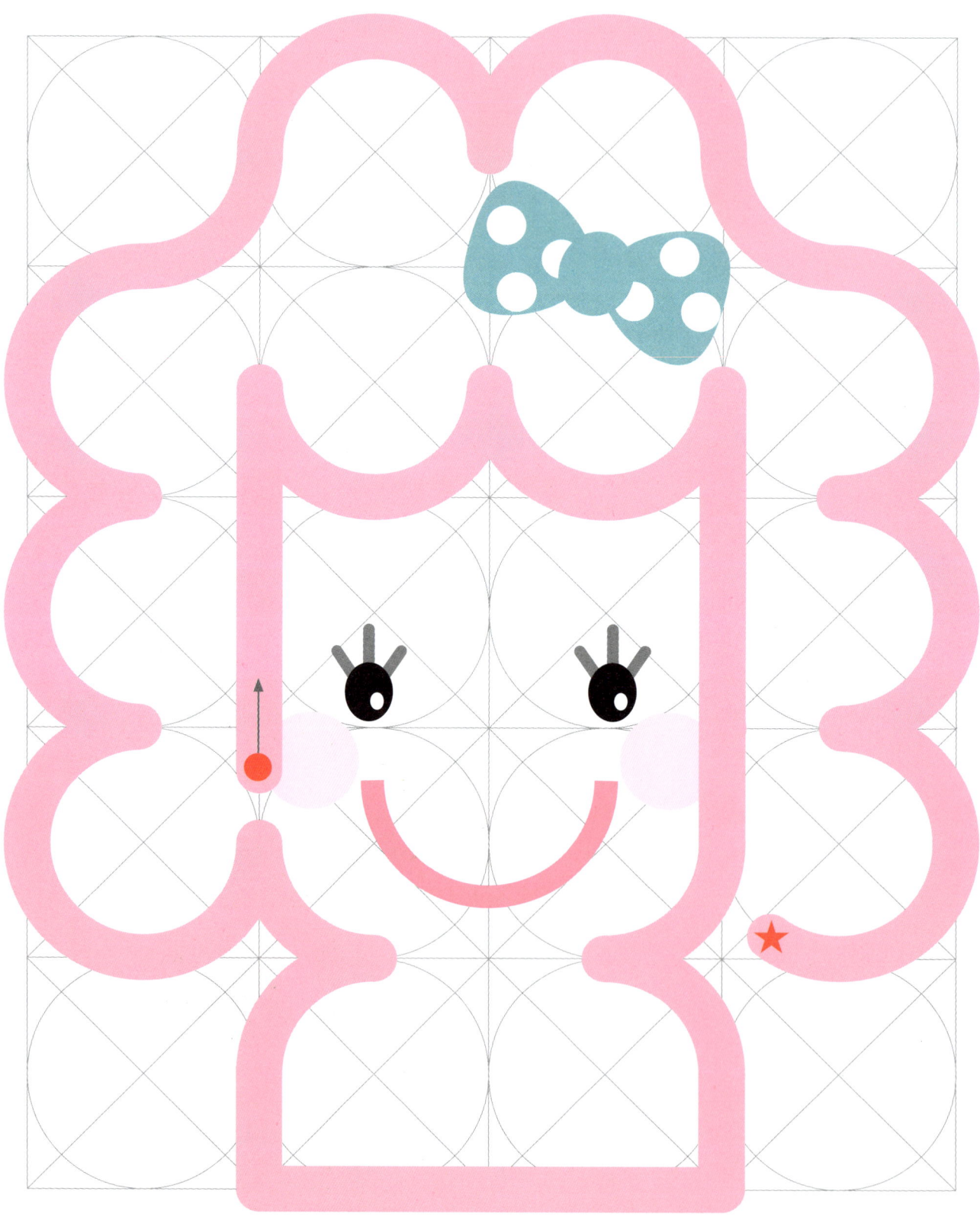

Curly Hair

23 Honeybees Buzz

Name

Date

- Draw a line from one bee (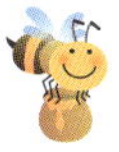) to the other bee (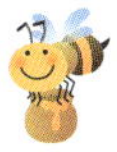).

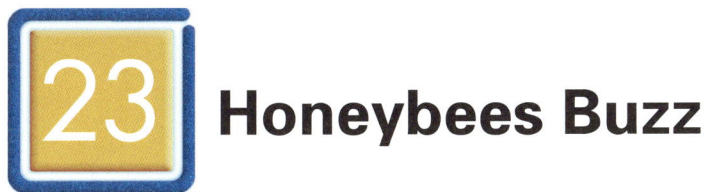

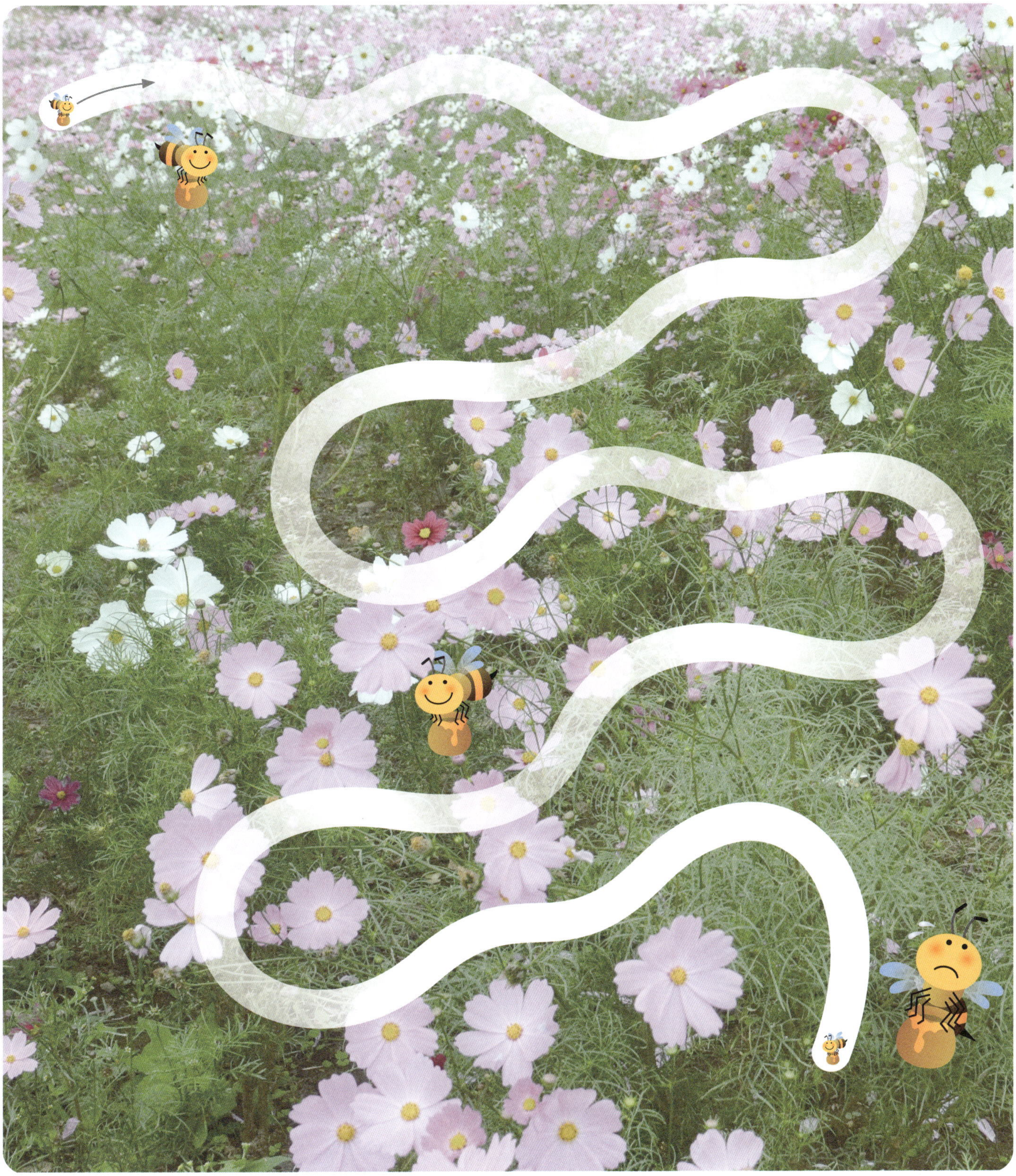

■ Draw a line from the dot (●) to the star (★).

Robot

24 Bubble Blast

Name
Date

■ Draw a line from one bubble wand (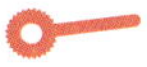) to the other bubble wand (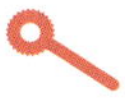).

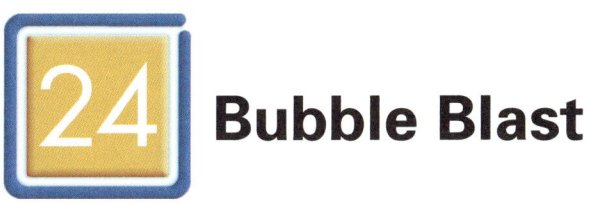

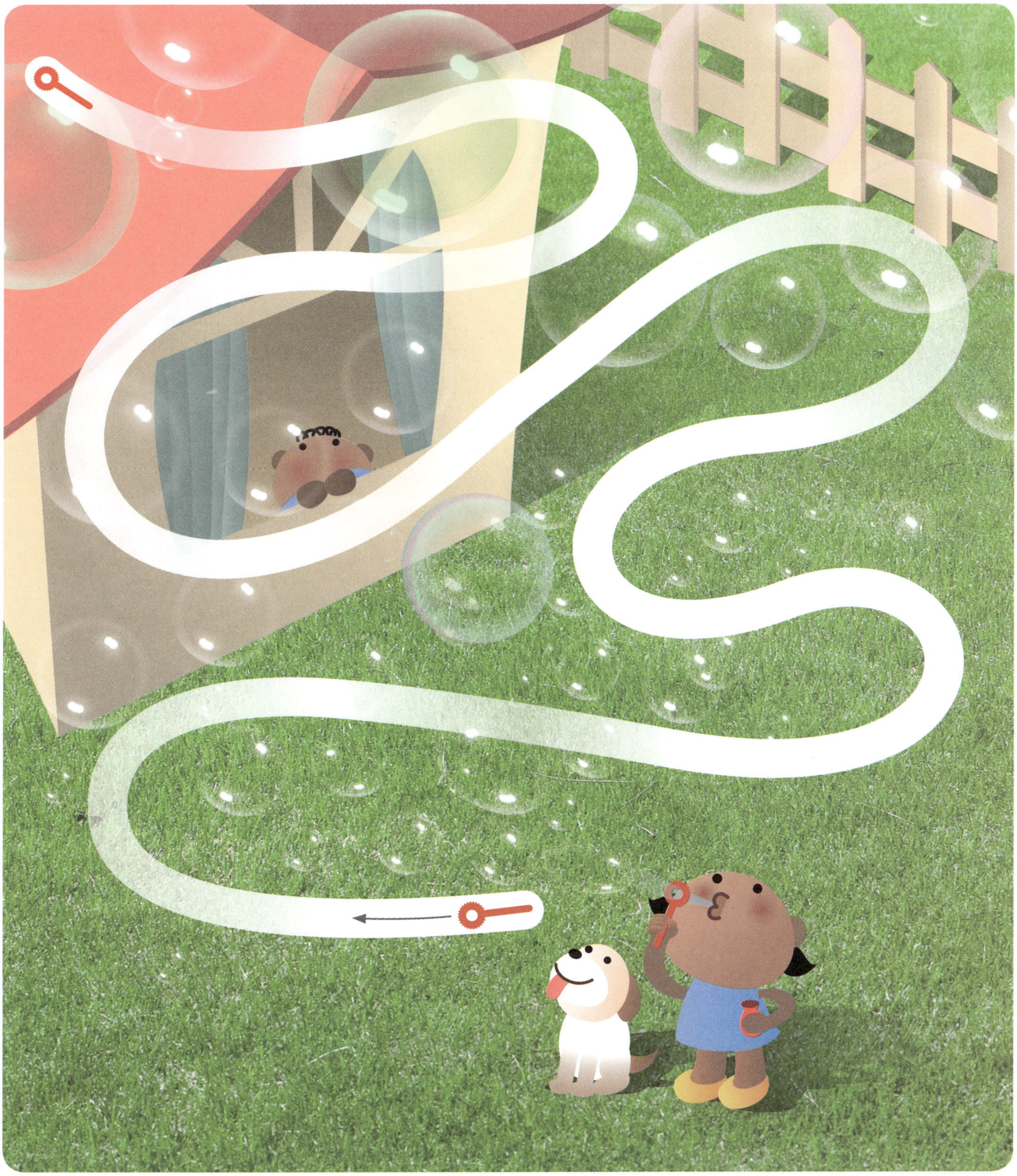

■ Draw a line from the dot (●) to the star (★).

Bakery

25 Sidewalk Chalk

Name

Date

To parents You can give your child hints if the exercise is too difficult. For example, you can tell him or her to trace the line with his or her finger first.

■ Draw a line from one chalk ( ) to the other chalk ( ).

■ Draw a line from the dot (●) to the star (★).

50

House

26 Moon Ride

Name

Date

■ Draw a line from one earth (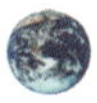) to the other earth (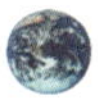).

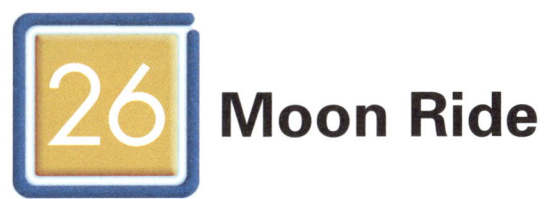

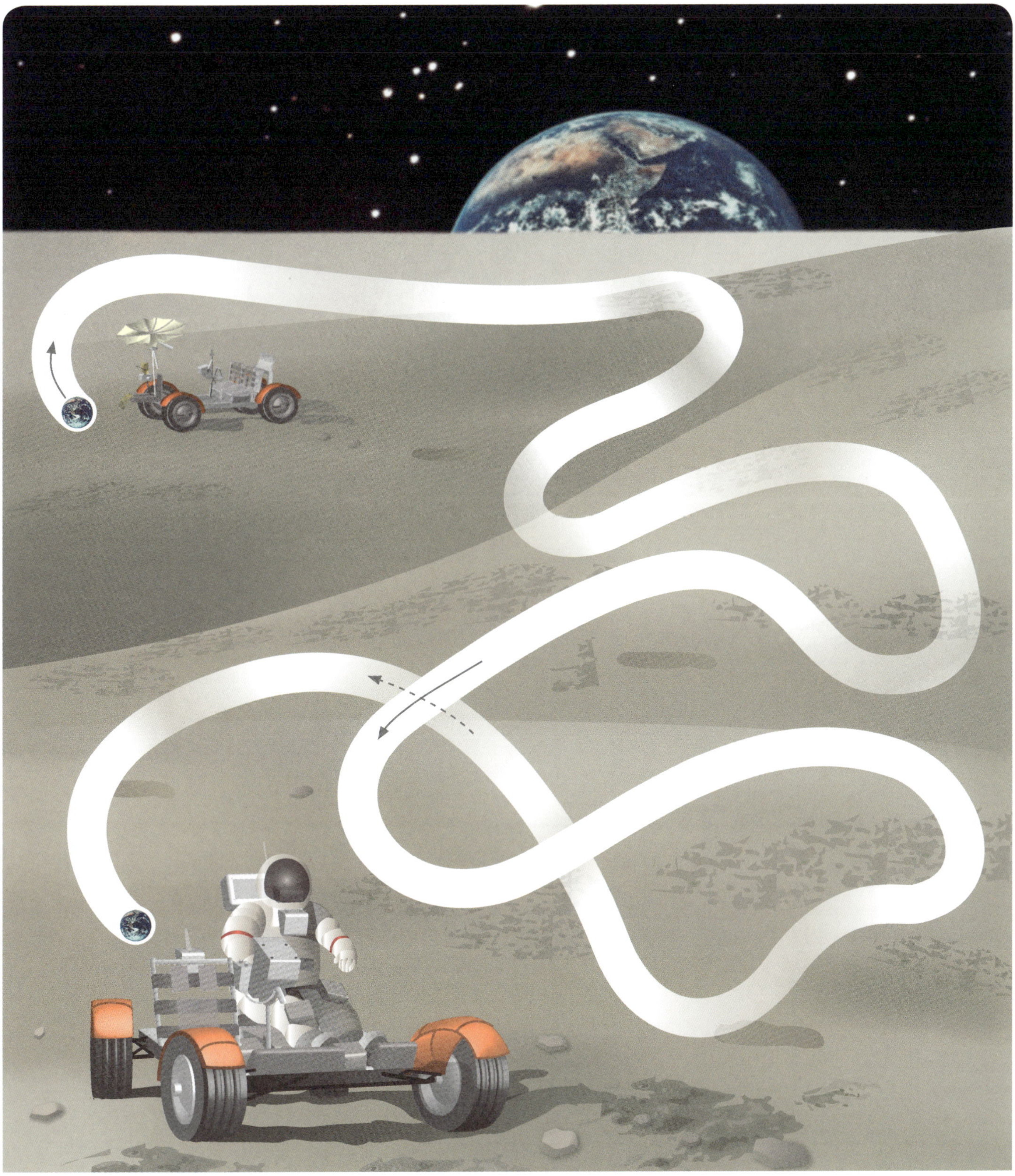

- Draw a line from the dot (●) to the star (★).

Ice-Cream Sundae

27 Golf Course

■ Draw a line from one golf ball () to the other golf ball ( ).

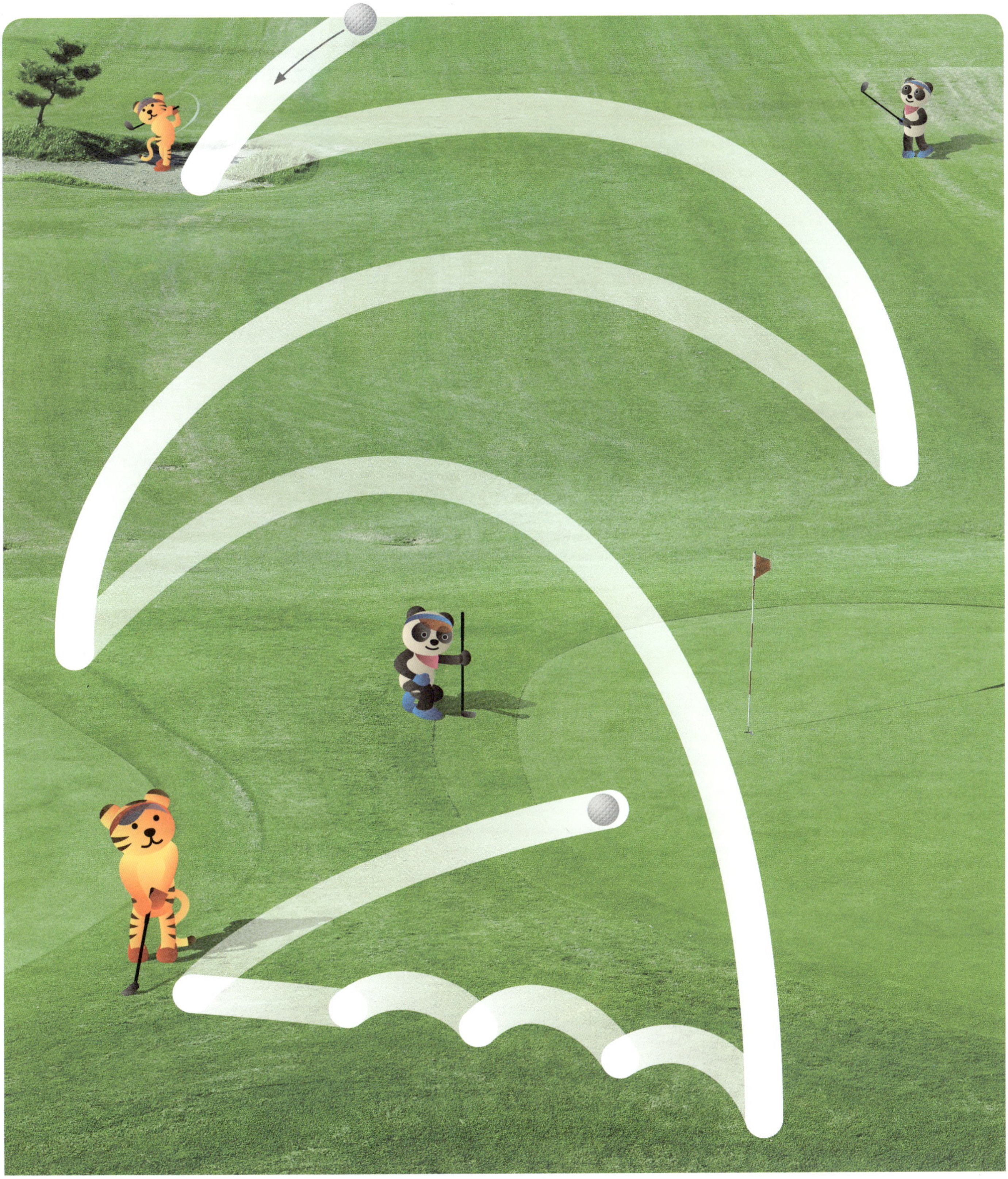

53

■ Draw a line from the dot (●) to the star (★).

Doll

28 Skate and Spin

Name
Date

■ Draw a line from one skate ( ) to the other skate ( ).

55

■ Draw a line from the dot (●) to the star (★).

29 Flying over the Field

Name
Date

To parents Encourage your child to draw the path of the dragonfly. If your child is unsure of the path, please ask him or her to trace the line with his or her finger first. When he or she has completed the exercise, offer lots of praise.

■ Draw a line from one dragonfly () to the other dragonfly ( ).

57

■ Draw a line from the dot (●) to the star (★).

Dinosaur

30 Fish in Flight

Name
Date

- Draw a line from one flying fish ( ) to the other flying fish ( ).

59

■ Draw a line from the dot (●) to the star (★).

Helicopter

31 Genie in a Bottle

Name
Date

To parents It is okay if your child draws outside the white area. The important thing is to encourage your child to draw slowly and carefully.

■ Draw a line from one lamp ( ) to the other lamp ( ).

61

■ Draw a line from the dot (●) to the star (★).

Backhoe

32 Pet Hedgehog

- Draw a line from one hedgehog () to the other hedgehog ( ).

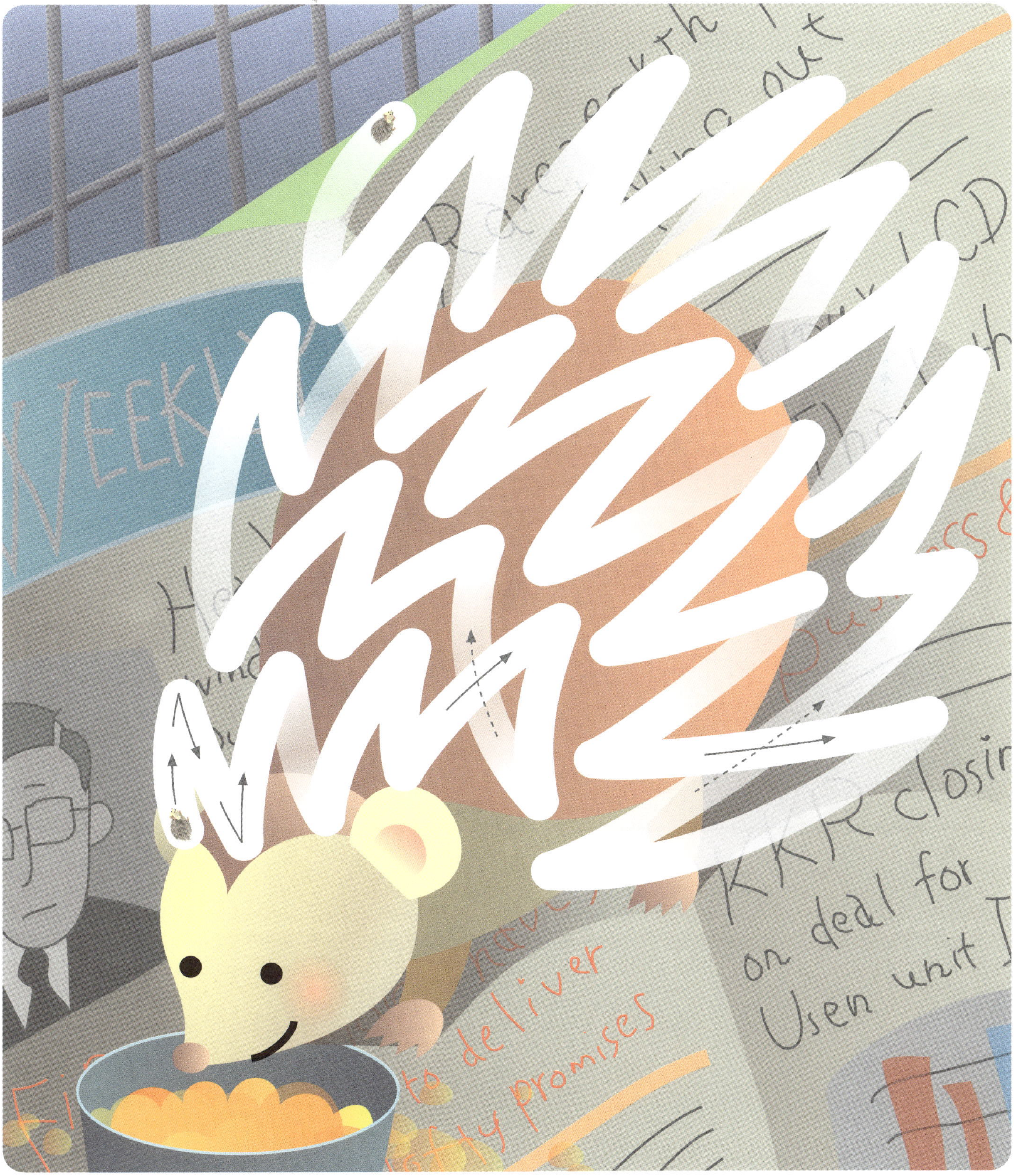

63

■ Draw a line from the dot (●) to the star (★).

Drummer

33 Rollercoaster Ride

Name

Date

■ Draw a line from one car (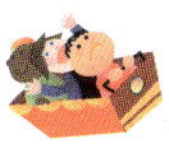) to the other car (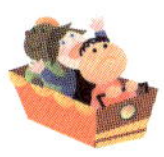).

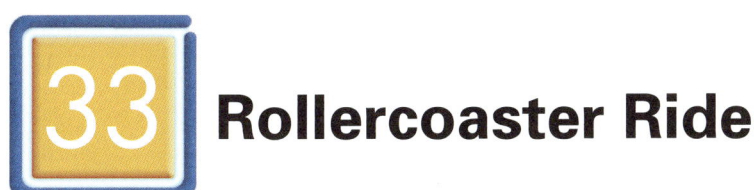

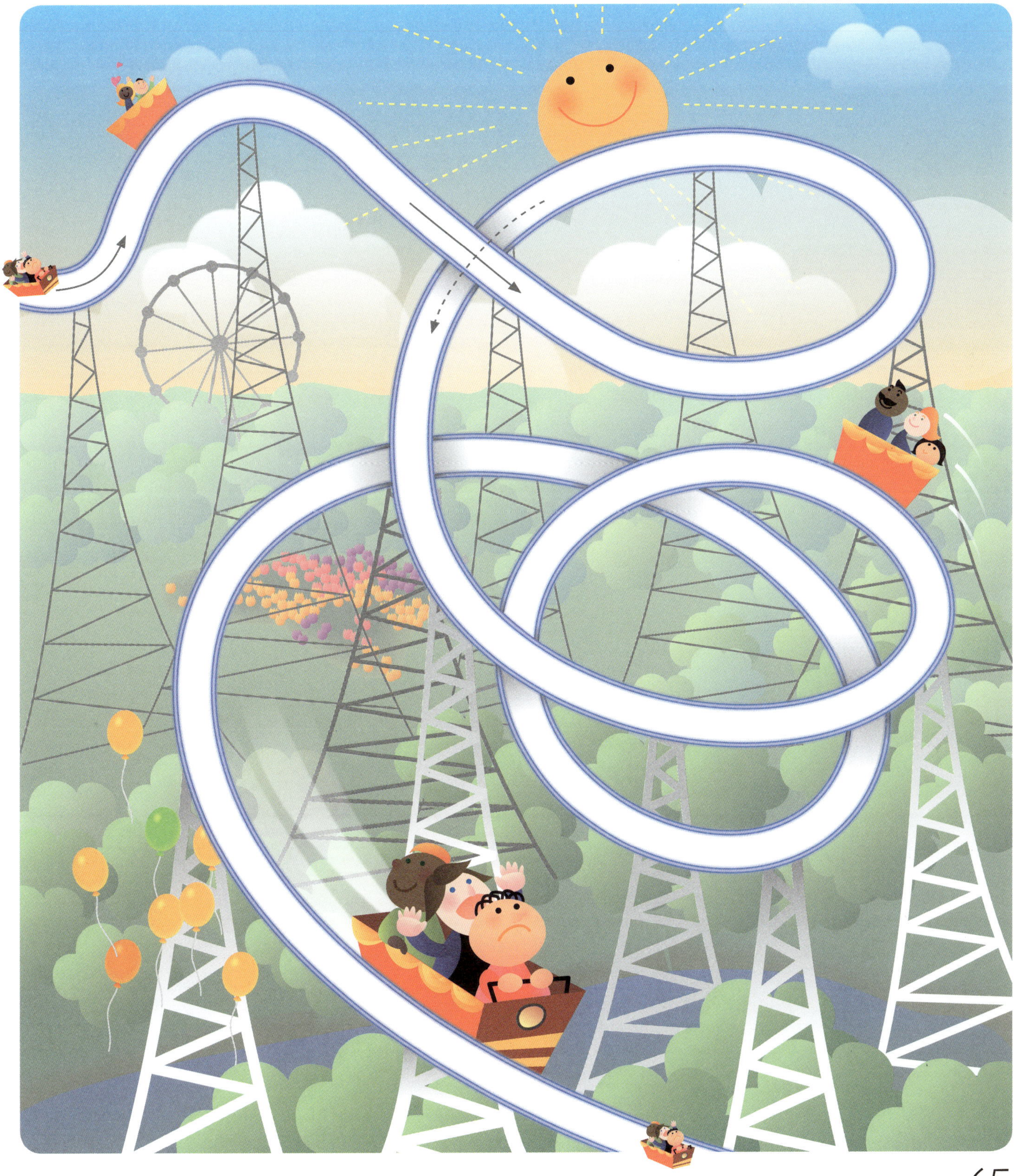

■ Draw a line from the dot (●) to the star (★).

Singer

34 The Big Bad Wolf

Name
Date

To parents Encourage your child to draw the path of the pig. Make sure your child follows the line at each crossing point so that he or she draws in the correct direction.

■ Draw a line from one pig ( ) to the other pig ( ).

67

■ Draw a line from the dot (●) to the star (★).

Cooking

35 Spaghetti Surprise

- Draw a line from one fork (🍴) to the other fork (🍴).

■ Draw a line from the dot (●) to the star (★).

Skateboarder

36 A Sunny Stroll

■ Draw a line from one hiker () to the other hiker ( ).

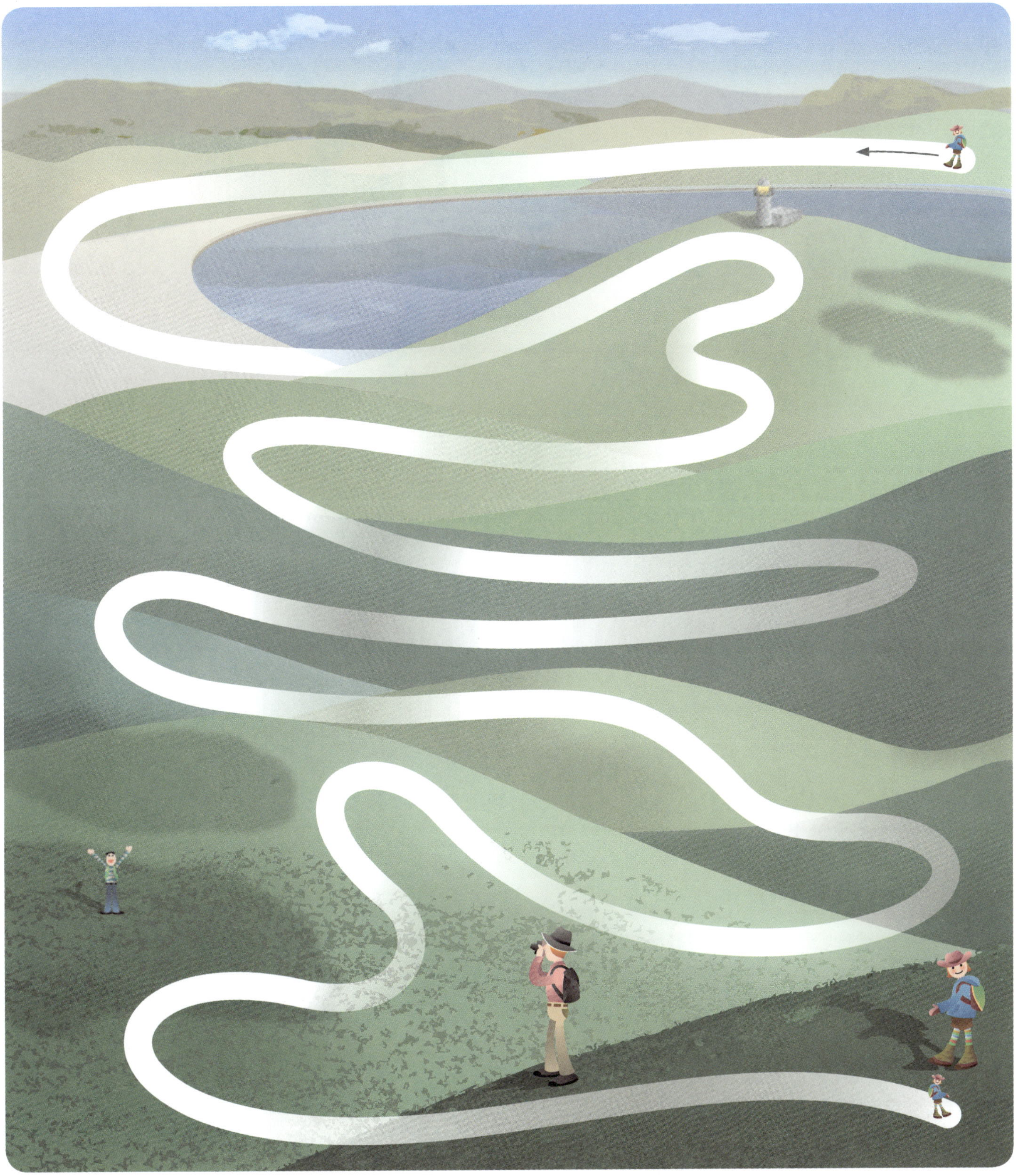

■ Draw a line from the dot (●) to the star (★).

Flowers

37 Freestyle

Name

Date

■ Draw a line from one board (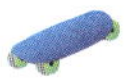) to the other board (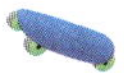).

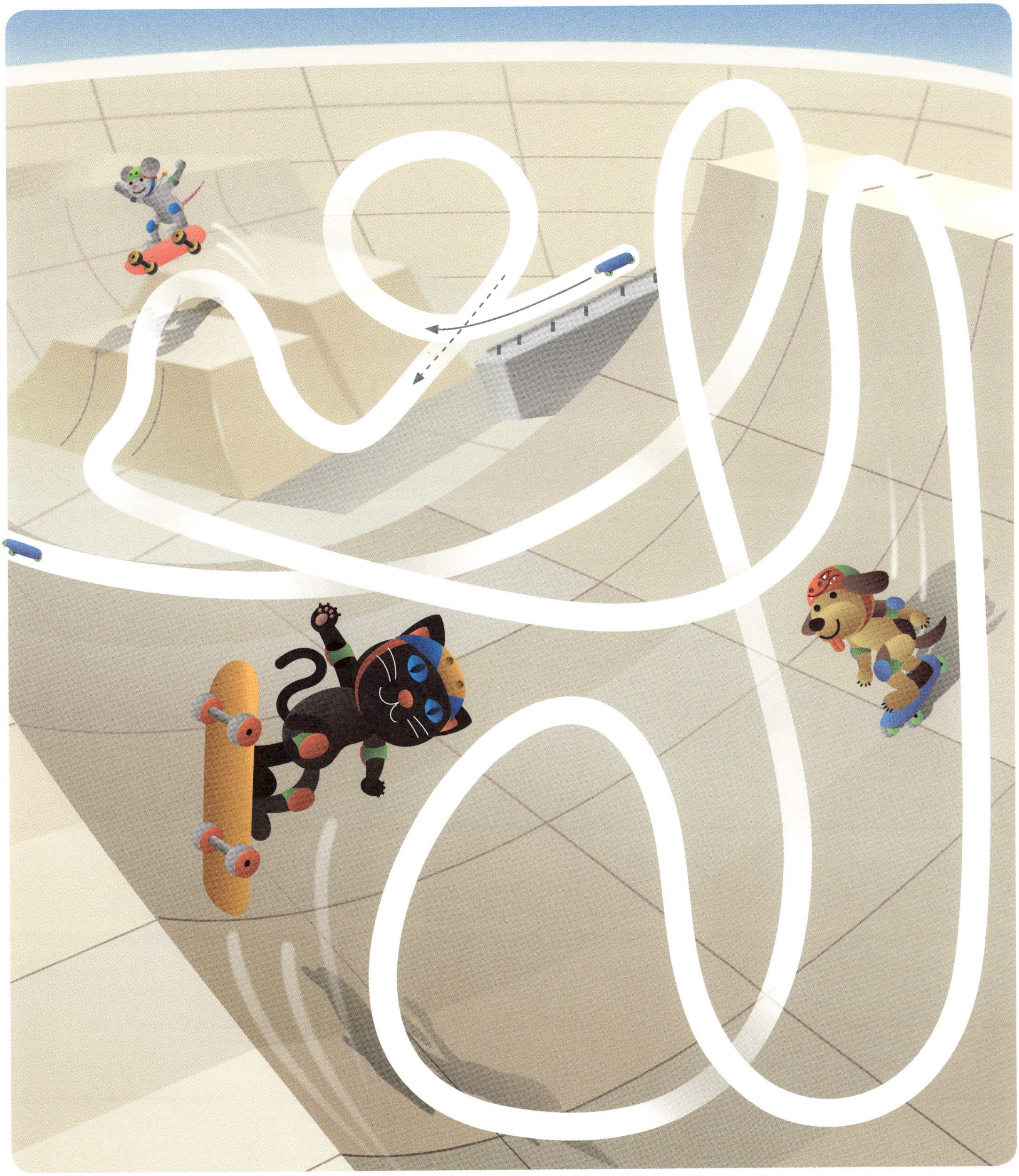

■ Draw a line from the dot (●) to the star (★).

Whale

38 Rollercoaster Rockies

Name
Date

To parents The path on this page is narrow. It is more important that your child draw slowly and carefully, rather than draw in one stroke. When your child has completed the exercise, offer lots of praise.

■ Draw a line from one car ( ) to the other car ().

■ Draw a line from the dot (●) to the star (★).

Pegasus

Certificate of Achievement

KUMON

_____

is hereby congratulated on completing

My Book of Amazing Tracing

Presented on _____, 20____

_____
Parent or Guardian

trace me